Loss and Language

Loss and Language

Jenny Robertson

Chapman Publications
1994

Published by
Chapman
4 Broughton Place
Edinburgh EH1 3RX
Scotland

The publisher acknowledges the financial assistance
of the Scottish Arts Council.

A catalogue record for this volume is
available from the British Library.

ISBN 0-906772-62-1

Chapman New Writing Series
Editor Joy Hendry
ISSN 0953-5306

Some of these poems have previously appeared in
*Chapman, Lines Review, Poetry North, Scottish Slavonic Review,
West Coast Poetry* and *Zed20*

Designed & typeset by Peter Cudmore

Cover design: Fred Crayk

Printed by
Mayfair Printers
Print House
William Street
Sunderland
Tyne and Wear

Contents

Contents

Preface

Beyond the Border was concerned with the borders which separate and define us, with a homeland whose landscape is words. *Ghetto* is an elegy to give voice to those who were silenced. A reviewer noted: "It is this intimate knowledge of a people who lost almost everything, including their heritage, which informs her poetry..." (Book Choice, The *Scotsman*, 1989). *Loss and Language* takes these themes further: Gaels were swept away from our shores in a holocaust which parallels the near total extinction of Yiddish-speaking Jewry. The collection begins with ten poems which follow the story of a place – Ardnamurchan. It moves to Orkney, to Poland whose poets – freedom fighters with words – retained the language, culture and national identity of their people even when the nation was wiped off the map of Europe in the nineteenth century and all but annihilated in the twentieth; to Russia, whose people experience loss and confusion as their country sheds its empire to re-emerge as a nation. Since loss is linked with restoration in the eternal paradoxes of our lives there are included some poems by pre-teen girls in Russia: a new generation whose poetic voice may yet shape Russia's future.

The poems also explore women's experiences of loss, restoration and language, including a sequence taken from the diary of Vibia Perpetua (c. 202AD), and the collection ends with a poem sequence about the loss of self as the result of a chronic illness.

Jenny Robertson's work in St. Petersburg has brought her to the point at which she has had to shed the Polish she feels deeply for, as well as her own language, and learn to clothe her thought patterns in Cyrillic shapes and sounds: a personal experience of loss and language.

Silhouette

The evening sun slants through glass
    to touch your hair.
Your mind is full of the sound of the sea.
You have glimpsed the shy otter
at the end of the rocks; have heard
seals sing, seen heron and curlew fly.

Soon you will stand against the horizon
    ringed with fire:
        an in-gathering of islands.

Ardnamurchan

The sky here is varied as the tide:
each ebb of wind
lifts cloud, pulls headlands clear of mist;
each flow birls rain against black rock,
drives lowering weather in,
unlocks a glow-worm blink of light
or fills the west with fire.

Tourists, summer-long,
disturb the skylark's liquid song,

do not know
the destitute
were forced to cut this ribbon route.

Malnourished mothers,
knitting pins in knotted hands,
bore creels of stones

while their men hewed back-breaking hours
for meagre pence

and bairns, accounted old enough and fit,
were also put to this roadwork.

"... but as they went they wept."

Now roads are built for speed
and sea and rock and sky,
that interplay of silence, sound and muted light,
bear no footprint
of those unshod folk,
no echo of their lost language,
no lament.

Rubha an Duin Bhain

The first tribe guarded the headland
with rough-bigged stones,
left, among blown dunes
scattered bones.

Wind, time and tide unravelled all they were:
their loyalties, their war,
their legends, laughter, lore.

The Question

Musicians came to the hall last night,
unpacking sagas and songs.
Harp music rippled like the burn in spate
baptising old battles and wrongs.

A boy slipped outside.
"King of the Mysteries, shall I leave
chariots and honour, passion and pride
for an uncertain boat and the sea's grey heave?"

Rocks raised question marks
on the parchment of the tide. "Who will make
this journey with me among currents and sharks?
King, Christ, will I take

your song in my coracle over the sea?
Will I rest with you as I lie at night
on birch without eiderdown? Hard sanctity!
Will I choose holiness without fame or delight

to build a church of driftwood and turf,
and preach to mackerel and gulls?
For the wave and for you, Bright King, leave the hearth,
the hall and the harp, the mead and the girls?

The Chief's Daughter

I am the chief's daughter.
The babies I bore died before they had names.

A king's son will lie with me, but I do not love him.

Today I turn my steps towards a hill where burn water runs
  seaward.
An Irish monk stands there, bare feet in bell-heather;
thralls all around him;
children tumbling together, wave-crests of children.

Buzzards wheel, mewing like kittens.

He is thin, this brother, his skin brown as leather. He speaks
  of a dove, of fire, of wisdom.

I leave my rock shelter, feel women assess my softness.

The monk's fingers fold like wings about me. Strength of
  high summer is in this ragged man's blessing.

I am the chief's daughter. I say: "You shall have a sheepskin
  to cover your shoulders, a jar of my own ale, venison, honey."

"Give them instead to these sisters and brothers..."

My arms encircle sour-smelling infants.

I will bring my king-partner a bride-gift of beggars.

Blind Mother

My house is in shadow, children move in endless dusk.
I feel holes in ragged garments, touch tangled hair.
I ask: "Is there meal in the kist?"
Six voices answer: "None".
I ask: "Is there water?"
A child holds a jar out to the rain.
I ask: "Is there oil in the cruisie?"
They tell me buttercups are brimful of sun.

Single Parent Family

1

He came to me in summer evenings
when light lingers long.

I led my brown heifer by the shore and sang.

Those sunlit days are gone.

2

My father, a godly man,
cannot countenance the black disgrace.
"It's the Parish for you now, lass."

I said, "The Parish will suffice."

My mother uttered one long moan.

I wept as I left my home.

3

I am brought to bed with twins.

The Session Clerk demands:
"Who fathered these bastard bairns?"
I say, "I never knew his name."
"No need," replied the tight-lipped man.
"You knew more than his name."

4

The boy is sickly. I sing a charm
to shield my bairns from strife and harm.

5

"Love is easy, love is light,
when summer's long and days are bright",
the doctor muses, takes his fee.
"Will your lad not share your shame,
give his name, accept the blame?"

This doctor does not know
your touch brought larksong from the sky,
gave me wonder, gave me worth:

gave me these twins I brought to birth.

6

I receive a groat, barley meal,
gather cockles in my creel.

Watch my bairns grow, pinched, thin.

I whisper your name when I pray.

Water brought you to me.
I have heard that water carried you away.

7

The news-sheet reports:

"In the Highlands they are preparing in almost every
quarter to go to America. Indeed, considering the extreme
scarcity, even bordering upon want, that prevails in many
districts, it is no wonder that emigrations should take place."

8

Water, says the spae-wife,
half a world wide, half a world long,
sunders kindred, birth-ties, song.

9

"Removal," says the laird's man, "is the means
to rid unprofitable land of feckless folk.
I am drawing up a list of those who cannot pay.
It were good," he adds, "to see
the remaining tenantry better lodged,
and I am under the impression, Miss..."
(Another man interprets, reckons, writes.)
"...that any payment *you* may make
will be very slight.
I am expecting you to emigrate."

The man – I will not utter his traitor name –
translates again.

I hear harsh words:
"Australia, gold mines,
opportunity, wealth."

10

I have lived here always
surrounded by wide skies and islands.

I know the good properties of flowers and berries.

My language rinses my mouth
like water pouring amidst sunlit hillsides
fragrant with thyme.

Now all this is ended.

Smoke stings my eyelids like tears.

My young ones in my arms,
and the taste in my mouth
bitter as hunger, salt as the sea.

Nature Study, 1910

School-children crossed bay and bog
with a crowdie piece, a well-cut peat
(that ancient mix of bog and heather root),
sometimes went out along the shore
for Nature Study, which may lend
more brightness than scratch of chalk on slate,
rhyming Dick Whittington, that lad o pairts –
and what's the use of golden streets
to bairns whose bare feet cross silver sand,
who watch white breakers rise and roar?

"Come, children!"
Miss Taylor's perfect English
lacks the music Gaeldom gives the Southern tongue.
"It is the flowering season. We must collect
our specimens, classify, select
watergowan, violet,
clover, heather, foxglove, broom,
return then to our own schoolroom,
draw our flowers, note each name."

Miss Taylor, reared in Morningside,
teaches children who will soon
serve maritime and landed wealth,
nurse, increase the Glasgow police,
leave the croft, the hill, the burn.

Miss Taylor recites Tennyson,
instructs in basic hygiene
girls whose great-grandmothers, illiterate,
could prepare
toad to heal dropsy, worm for gout,
boil shell-fish, cormorant, limpet
to fill the flesh of thin changelings:

there are no children in that schoolhouse now.

Old Parish Kirk

The place where people prayed is overgrown
with grass and thistle, a neglected shell
where criss-cross ivy buttresses thick stone:
a scaffolding of branch and leaf and wall.

Exposed to gale and sun on its green hill,
this roofless kirk keeps always open door.
Three glassless windows face the Sound of Mull;
dense weeds, knee-high, invade, in hordes, its floor.

To build the kirkyard, stonework was displaced
and buried here, the landlord's hated tool.
"When you are dead," a homeless woman cursed,
"let nettles prove the devil has your soul."

The tacksman's grave bears witness to that doom:
land and kirk are barren as his tomb.

Parish Kirk, Contemporary

So John and Morag bring their babe to kirk
to be baptised; and sea and sky wear lace
to mark the day. Cars back and queue to park,
for birth shows continuity of place,
and pews are packed, though galleries are blocked
where minister and gentry once were raised
above douce Sunday-suited crofting folk.
Today the child, sign in which we trace
our source, is in the midst: all white and pink
she yells as water drops upon her face –
to great goodwill. She is a living link
whose name is in the Gaelic of her race
which kirk and commerce can no longer think:
the heritage is hers, as hers the grace.

Soundings of Silence

When the tongue tires
        let the wind
pare language to the bone;

commerce be exchanged
for the symphony of seabirds and tide

where roads scale down into footpaths
crossing headland and moor.

A glimmer of grey, or blue
        at each turning
carries the focus to far horizons

and back full circle to seek
        the intersection
of quest and the unfathomable

soundings of silence:
        locus both
of voyage and sojourn in harbour.

Viking Brooch, Rousay

Although the dead cannot hear
they buried her with the sound of the sea in her ear;

dressed her in kirtle and sark with skill and care,
fastened brooches she favoured for festive wear.

Silvered gold, slender pin, rich interlace
shone beneath her motionless face.

They brought her infant, dead at its birth;
shrouded mother and child with stone and earth.

Centuries unravelled clothing and flesh,
unstitched the bairn on the withered breast,

until a plough struck against a burial stone,
uncovered rare gold gleaming on a knotwork of bone.

Her jewellery was taken, classified, assessed,
ticketed, displayed behind casing and glass.

Her grave is hidden by thistle and grass
where the sea's requiem enfolds her and cloud shadows pass.

Grandmother from Stronsay

In her round hat, lisle stockings,
lace-up shoes, long coat, she bought
good butcher meat
from Glasgow shops mizzled with rain and soot.
Those grey streets, shawled women, rattling trams,
bundles of washing trundled to the steamie in prams
were a world away
from the seven-mile stretch of ribbon road
which threads her island home.
At eighty she climbed fences,
longed to kick her height
as her own grandmother had done
in that faraway place of shifting light
we visited in the tales she told.
Her vowels sang;
and when friends came
she pulled her pinny on,
baked pancakes, girdle scones, soft, warm.
Stripped to her semmit and her petticoat
her body was as lean as her northern sun,
her frame as enduring as the weathered stone
which built the farm where she was born.

Stronsay Knitwear

Aggie knits yarns. Her tales spin
more swiftly than swoop of whitemaa or tern
on eddies of wind.
Her talk, like her knitwear, has a design all her own.

She patterns flowers of sound on the wing:

tells of a wife whose room was so damp
the paper was flapping loose from the wall,
and "the peedie mice cam peeping from holes in the floor."

Aggie's tale repeats like shapes on gloves and yokes:
one row plain, purl, pass wool over, slip one, start again.

The old woman wouldn't leave her mould or her mice,
but her family stepped in.
"I didn't go near," says Aggie, "for I couldna bear
to watch them tak her away on the plane,
but she knew what was afoot when I never came."

Aggie's needles cast on wool of a new colour and tone.
She returns to her yarn. By the time it is done
the mice are running across the piano, playing a tune.

24

Unicorn

No eagle poised on straining wings,
brash and bronze against the dim
fold of rainwashed skies,
against the bleat of new-dropped lambs:

Scotland's symbol is the unicorn:
a beast of dream, ox-strong and slim,
whose creamy shoulders broke an early dawn
before walls were raised or makars born.

A beast of fable with its single horn,
fey and fearsome; yet will come
to a girl's untutored song,
lay its crested head, like blossom, down:

a gentle guardian of frailty,
dumb as moonlight, potent, free.

Runrig, Edinburgh

The castle walls are drowned in drifts of haar;
high-voltage lights flash sharp as raised claymores:
the wheel which turns our years spins songs, not war

while Wallace, Bruce keep guard for evermore.
We sing "Alba!" beneath their silent stare:
the word drowns castle walls like rolling haar.

The wheel which turns our years spins songs, not war.
The castle keeps love-locks – a Prince's hair;
preserves, unworn, the crown of Scotland here

where lasers flash lights bright as raised claymores.
What redcoat, laird laid waste these songs restore:
now Gaelic drowns old walls like drifting haar;

for thousands dance and clap and sing and cheer
where Wallace, Bruce still stare through coloured haar.
High-voltage lights flash sharp as raised claymores.
The wheel which turns our years spins songs, not war.

Freedom Fighters

(translated from *Dziady* (Hallowe'en), a verse play by Poland's national poet, Adam Mickiewicz (1833). When the play was performed by a student theatre group in Warsaw on the eve of the freedom movements of the 1980s, the authorities tried to suppress performances.)

A crowd surrounded the prison like a motionless rampart;
two ranks of soldiers stood like a ceremonial parade from the
    palace right to the prison gates with weapons and guns and
    those transport carts right in the midst. I took another look.
That's the police commander getting on his horse –
a great man in charge of a great triumph:
the triumph of the Czar, the victor of the North over children!
Then I saw them. Each one was followed by guards with
    bayonets.
Just boys! Reduced to absolute poverty, bareheaded like
    recruits, only with shackles on their legs.
Poor boys! The youngest, barely ten, complained that he
    couldn't drag the chain along.
So the police chief rides up, asks what's wrong.
The police chief – a humane fellow – inspects the chain:
"Ten pounds – that's all right, it's the official weight."
They took students too.
I saw one I knew, trying to cheer the others up,
he smiled at the crowd, saying goodbye with a bitter look,
    but kind.
He shook his chain to show it didn't weigh him down too much,
and as the cart pulled away, he took off his cap, stood up
and shouted three times: "Poland isn't lost yet!"
The crowd gathered round him, but for a long time
you could still see that hand pointing to the sky,
the hat, black as a funeral banner,
and his head, with the hair shamelessly torn out.
That head was unashamed, proud, visible from afar,
proclaiming its innocence and ignominy for everyone to see.
That hand and that head remained in my sight
and stay in my mind still, guiding my life,
pointing like a compass to show where virtue lies.
If I forget them, God in heaven,
forget me too...

To a Polish Mother

(written in 1830 by Adam Mickiewicz, this poem looks beyond
despair, slavery, martyrdom to national renewal and has passed
into Poland's literature and language as a statement of personal
worth which transcends both loss and freedom.)

Look into your son's eyes, O Polish mother:
if any gleam of genius sparkles there:
if pride, the legacy of his forefathers
marks that young forehead crowned with childish hair;

if he discards his own companions
and lends a willing ear to old men's tales
of daring deeds and long-dead champions
and his ardent attention never fails –

Polish mother, wrongly your son has played!
Kneel before our Mother of Sorrows,
see the sword which made her bleed:
the foe will pierce you too with painful blows.

No matter if the world blossoms with peace,
your son's destiny is crucifixion;
though allied nations declare that war will cease,
his call is death and martyrdom, not resurrection.

So from his earliest childhood bid him go
alone with day-dreams to his serpent's lair,
there spread his mat woven of fresh willow
and breathe the foul and putrid air.

He'll learn to hide his anger underground,
keep thought well-hidden in a deep abyss,
be lowly, silent, for vile fumes surround
his speech, polluted by the viper's kiss.

In Nazareth our young redeemer played
with tiny crosses, toyed with future pain:
Polish mother, make your child unafraid,
give him his future toys, an iron chain

to wreathe his infant wrists, then harness him,
small slave-labourer, to his wheelbarrow.
Now he won't flinch when axes threaten him;
the hangman's rope won't freeze his marrow.

He won't ride on crusade like knights of old
to save Jerusalem, nor sail to plough
New Worlds with freedom, shed his blood like gold.
Some unknown spy will send a challenge now

to wage war with a court which violates
the name of justice on a battlefield
underground, where the strong foe hates
and passes judgement on him, makes him yield.

Vanquished, his only monument
will be a wooden gallows;
his glory just a woman's brief lament
and night-long conspiracies of fellow-Poles.

Threnodies

A sequence of elegies by the father of Polish literature,
Jan Kochanowski (1530–84), express the poet's grief at the
death of his daughter. These elegies, constructed in a
variety of forms, including the first use of the sonnet in
Poland, constitute a psychological drama which charts the
processes of grief. The poems which follow are an attempt
to distil Kochanowski's poetic thought, compressed from
the original nineteen poems.

1

I hoped to pass my lute to you,
my songstress small,
who brightened our Slavonic woods,
shy nightingale,
early delighting listening hearts,
now choked with tears.
Did this legacy seem light to you
who play with stars?

"Farewell, my mother, bless me now",
so sings the bride.
"I leave your table, kitchen, hall
for my husband's side."

Daughter, embroidered robes and skirt
await in vain.
You chose instead a linen shift,
a narrow home.
I bind laces, beads about your waist
and shining hair,
and close within an oaken chest
dowry and heir.

2

Where are you hiding, my daughter?
Europe is wide. Where shall I seek?
Have you become a child-angel,
visited far, happy isles?
Does Orpheus sing to you?
Has the boatman of shades led you
to the waters of memory loss
where no mortal tears may flow?
Was there found some small stain
of impurity in your childish frame?
O, unworthy I, bowed with grief
to follow your bright steps to that holy purging!
Wherever you are, have pity on me.
Visit my sleepless bed – like a dream.
Comfort my waking – like a sunbeam
casting your shadow into the house,
so full of us, so empty of you:
so small a daughter, so large a space.

3

O waesome myth, o waefu wife,
whose dule dirls in storm and rain.
Her bairns lie streeked like corn in hairst.
She dwines and stiffens to a stane.
Within the rock she has become
her tears warsel yet, a hidden sea
and hurl in spate
for herd and gangrel, beast and wean:
her sorrow may their saining be.

4

I see that sorrow may a blessing be,
but Wisdom now exacts a bitter fee;
holds love and joy as dross, requires one mind
in fortune as in lack. Mentor unkind!
I strove for years, spent youth and wealth, to glimpse
your portals, reach your palace steps; and since
I climbed this high, you throw me low, to learn
like Cicero, who counselled calm, to mourn
is not a crime, for we are flesh, not stone.
Our wounds want balm. Philosophy alone
deceives, for all must grieve. Distracted thought
pure reason spurns when hope deserts the heart.

Impious death thus desecrates each shrine
once sacrosanct, which I deemed vainly mine.

5

Death desecrates each holy place:
philosophy, reason, even grace
are nullified by one dire blow.

In this we see your hand, O Lord.
Hope withdrawn is scourging hard,
a rod to make us rebels grow

more worthy of our Father's care,
who turn reluctantly to prayer,
preferring pleasures found below.

Sir, punish me: it is your right,
but gently too. Before your sight
I must melt like summer snow.

In this my hope: the world will fade
before you spurn a soul you made.
Kind Lord, show pity; show
love surpassing human woe.

6

At dawn today I dreamt
my mother came with my daughter, dressed
in linen as I saw her last,
her face flushed, her eyes alight
as if she'd run from her cot
to lisp her bright paternoster.

"Did you think us lost?
Do you think no sunshine lights the dead,
that the spirit is less noble than the flesh?
See, your beloved child plays
among angels, she lit this morning's star.
Why look amazed?
Master, return to school!
Time heals. Don't reject this common cure.
Give former pleasures place once more;
reach forward, prepare
your heart for good or ill.
Human fortune humanly bear."

She ceased, was gone.
Another morning has begun.

Translations from Young Polish Poets

Andrzej Jastrzab

born 1969; prizewinner in the 8th Poznan Poetry Competition,
has published three collections of his work

Ring

a ring red like golden fever
shone on the finger
of the monarch dethroned on the scaffold
a dream white as opium pierced the cheers
of the crowd yelling
the king is dead, long live the republic
i was reborn that day
felt a flame warm
as the touch of a woman's breast

Katyn

before they dug open earth's swollen belly
bearing white skulls torn apart by the pressure of steel
a wall of unrest divided
the living from their lost comrades-in-arms

before questions about Katyn fell
in the misty fabric of guesses
assurances sent from the square of red roses
denied that Pilsudski's *sanacja* officers had been held prisoner

pine trees bent crowns of sorrow
and with amber tears embraced
eagles buried in the earth's coffin

Anna Czujkowska

born 1959; studied Pedagogics and Psychology,
sings, writes poems, composes, draws

Signs

When hours grow cold
i kneel
gather darkness about me
swing on the last thread of light
say the rosary
your letters my Lord
who art
        because all your signs
are on slips of paper
on the nape of my neck
        your lips
on my breasts
        your hands

Magdalena Samsel

born 1972; a pupil at Poznan Lyceum, she won recognition
in two poetry competitions in 1989

With a crochet hook
I make an extract
            Of memories

With the wind
I light in a whisper
            Of dreams

Life
Travels in green
            Sadness

To the stop by the cemetery
But there's room
            In heaven

To Celebrate Zhivago's Appearance in its Homeland

You took us to new frontiers, opened doors.
The curtain lifts. We come out on the stage.
A child howls, sign of our lost age;
a candle burns, two shadows cross, two stars.

Illumined by that single candle flame
dark worlds are brought together. Magdalene
embraces terror's tortuous machine
where lovers part without address or name.

With snow for tears she sows her Paschal fruit.
A birch tree hangs its shawl – an inspiration –
against a snowbound, starving station:
that year ripe wheat was left to rot uncut.

Though love intoxicates when famine stalks
your story sings: an unseen angel walks.

At the Graveyard of St. Seraphim

(St. Seraphim of Sarov is one of Russia's favourite saints. In St.
Petersburg a cemetery dedicated to the wartime dead bears his name.)

Birches rise, bare as bones,
crowded close as housing blocks.
The dead are also crowded here, their graves
fenced in: communist and priest,
doctor, artist; Russian, Hebrew names:
officers with medals carved on shiny slabs;
photographs of husband, daughter, wife;
plastic flowers, red stars, Slavonic cross.
Flags wave above the wartime dead.
A board proclaims: Immortal Leningrad.

Solemnities sealed these graves.
Snow shrouds them each long· winter. Spring stirs slow sap.
Summer brings citizens in search of living things.
Autumn shakes out leaves like silenced bells.

There is a presence here.
St. Seraphim has left his name,
and in his wooden church
God is served by those who come to stare,
and those who bow
their foreheads to the uncomplaining ground,
and fill their holy place
with the gentle light
of many candle flames.

The Prayer Rope

I wear prayer on my finger.
Natasha made the rope,
sitting up all night.
Four threads, twelve knots;
each knot takes seventeen twists,
winding silk around your fingers,
drawing loops into a cross,
passing one under the next –
the task requires care and skill,
focus; mind and body stilled.

Natasha lives in a high-rise block,
nowhere for herself, no space.

I twist her knots,
knit prayer on threads,
an endless circle on a finger ring.

Sankt-Peterburg

Queues massive and still as oaks
wait at dawn and dark.

Snow films unlit roads with ice.

A car skids to a stop. A child is flung,
too shocked to cry.

Dark forms shout, harangue.

The driver, young, gathers the boy
into his arms, drives on.

Headlights pinprick the sleet:

their gleam is thin as a wolf's winter eyes.

Still Life, St. Petersburg

Asters, roses on our table,
pink petals clustered round green stems,
framed by double panes of darkening glass,
bend in their vase
amidst a scatter of papers, coffee pots and pens.

From the school yard below
comes laughter: an unseen group of girls.

A last island of light fades behind a golden dome;
caught within a latticework of leaves
a slab of silver gleams: the harvest moon.

December 25th, St. Petersburg

From our window level with tree tops
I watch a brief December day
fade behind black branches.

Crows clamour – dark shapes – about a golden dome.

(A world away cities are sated with commerce
called, too crudely, Christmas.)

The tide of light has turned
with the midwinter solstice.

This frozen land is fasting;
its ill-lit streets poor showcases
for goods guarded as once the Tsar's gold glitter:

unreachable

as stars from a stable door.

Old Communist

His life has shrunk to a single room
among tall birches in a housing block.
His daughter, grand-daughter share their home,
divide their living-space to let him have his own
filled with the mindings of an ordered life
when men led women in bed and dance.
He went to war in Leningrad, Murmansk.
A year he hid in gloom
of forests; hands and well-drilled wits tracked tanks;
eighteen, then, prepared to die.
The leader, Lenin, broods above his bed.
This is no Peter to forswear or run away
though cock-crow heralds an uncertain day
and President, media, the young betray
his iron dream. Alert amidst the loss
his blue eyes laugh as with his guests
he downs a bottle, glass by glass.
A photograph? He smiles, combs back the hair
waving banner-bright about his head.

Among snores and slow talk on an endless train
with paper he has cut for cloths I spread
my table – with his salt eat fragrant bread.

Leaving Russia, Hogmanay

We drive through boundaries
        controlled by watch towers
                miles of barbed wire
sand pitted with mines.

                Snow girdles silent pines.

                Our headlights find
no colour,   no wayside cheer
                in this winter wilderness
the last day of the year.

We think: no herald runs
                no heaven-sent swans
        level the trackless sky with wing-beat sound,
        uttering, unearthly cry, angelic songs –
                no guiding star.

We leave a wasted land, vast goldfish bowl
        whose sides, once painted black,
                are pasted now with dollar bills.

                It is safer to depend
on the bully boy who guards a gangster chief
                than on the praises of a friend.

Suddenly: a barrier drops

We wind windows down   feel icy air
        Mother Russia's last caress...
What now? Documents? Bribes to let us pass?
        The boy is very young, on duty at this dark frontier:
brown eyes beneath his round fur hat, an edging of dark hair.
        "I come to wish the best
                Happy New Year!"
Our hands clasp.   He lifts the barrier.

        The way is clear.

Son of Man

His face is crowned with candleshine,
solemnity of soaring voices,
the incense word: *pomiluj.*

He is slumped in dust
of six million trampling feet,
hat of rabbit-fur askew.

Out of town we glimpse him among birches –
those naked Russian darlings –
reaching from thawing earth to distant blue.

Dark pines praise him,
bowed beneath April snow.

He is in the faces
of shawled women,
whose eyes suffer, bloodshot, bruised.

As well as in laughter of lovers
and children, swaddled like bundles
in soul-less cities, shabby and subdued.

Reverie

(after a painting by Pavel Tchistiakov, 1832–1919:
Giovanina seated on the window sill, 1864, Russian Museum)

Her eyes tranquil with reveries, a girl
muses, becalmed. The sky's oyster shell
beyond rooftops reveals its luminous pearl.
Her window is open to the first glimmer of dawn.
She is morning's sentinel: vigilant on the sill
she watches, not distant vistas, nor shadows below,
nor mists, drifting, dissolving – her gaze is within,
guarding thoughts all her own. She does not know
her reflection shimmers, mirror-like in the pane,
against which her shoulders repose. Seated so,
she is glimpsed by a painter, early astir,
who spreads out his canvas to capture her dream.

Translations of Poems by
St. Petersburg Schoolchildren

Fairy Story

Somebody comes quietly to me,
carefully takes hold of me,
Carries me on the wind
to that land of which I dreamt.

That planet is like a circle,
not at all large,
but I understood at once
that here love is in everyone.

One of the people who dwell on this planet
invited me to visit him.
He took me to the edge of the planet,
and we had a little talk by moonlight.

He poured out hot tea for me
and said, looking at me,
"Fly here, I'm bored without you.
I need you here, my dear!"

So, looking at the stars,
we lost count of time,
but I'd like to come back again and again.

Zhenya, age 12

The icon of the Vladimir Mother of God

There's so much love in you,
so much tender sorrow,
a heavy and sad look.
You consent to your cruel fate.
Where do your thoughts live,
and where do they fly to.
Do they fly to God
or do they find shelter here?

Rowans

Clusters of crimson rowans, catch fire soon!
Don't allow the light of sunny days to fade.
You will fill the earth with your burning warmth,
And from all nature cast off gloom.

Evgenia, age 12

Spring

Spring has come
the snow has melted,
water flows from rooftops,
and a little boy –
    a gnome –
    builds his home,
and starts to live there.

At the seaside

On Poseidon's birthday
mermaids decorated the sea
with a star which burns alone in the sky,
and with children's tears...

only nymphs who have died
and lie at the bottom of the sea were silent.

Asya, age 11

The Diary of Perpetua

Vibia Perpetua, a twenty-year-old mother, breast-feeding her child, was arrested for civil disobedience (c. 202 AD). She and her friends, including her pregnant slave, Felicitas, refused to perform the ritual for the Emperor's welfare and were sentenced to fight with beasts in the arena – a wild cow was sent against the two women.

Choice

My family bring violets,
weeping, heart-wrung pleas;
call me atheist, unnatural, strange.
I cannot change,
no, not for violets,
or memories of shadowed grass,
of birdsong, blossom, spring;
not even for my little son
– oh, nurse him well!

You say, abjure that impious braggart
dragging wretched wood, that slave,
his empty title slung around his neck.
But I say laurel wreaths
are mere profanities.
So do not tempt me now
with tears, or petals
soft as my baby's skin.

The bowstring of my choice is fully drawn.
Like a runner, stripped, oiled,
I speed arrow-swift towards my prize,
and only angels hear my feathers sing.

Her first prison dream

I entered a garden
filled with light,
with many thousands gathered,
dressed in white;
and, milking sheep, a pale-haired shepherd
fed his lambs.
His garb was coarse, his welcome kind:
"Child, come!"
He put some cheese into my hands:
"Daughter, eat!"
I ate the cheese the shepherd offered.
Its taste was sweet.
And, when I awoke, I still felt sweetness
on my breath.
At once I called my brother to me:
"It will be death."
From then we hoped no more for pleasure
in this life;
instead, having tasted heaven
I found health,
and though my father would not let me nurse my child
my breasts were not sore,
nor was I tormented with worry for him:
I hurt no more.

She dreams she fights the fiend

I heard knocking, urgent, loud,
the prison gates opened. I went
over rough rocks to a vast arena,
an astounded crowd; heard a voice speak to me alone:
"I shall share your fight."
I could not see who spoke

And now I saw my opponent:
no beast – a man, hideous, huge,
with fighting men beside him. I had companions too,
young men who stripped and oiled me.
I knew no shame, for I became a man.

And now the Master came – a tower, tall. He wore the purple,
sandals were trimmed with silver, tied with gold.
He bore a green bough laden with golden apples:
"This will be your prize: now fight."

I struck the fiend's face with my heels,
trampled him to shouts of triumph, victory songs.
Then the Master took my face between his hands:
"Daughter, peace!" I received his kiss, received
the apple bough: and woke.

I have recorded the main events since our arrest.
I cannot record the contest. If anyone
wishes to do so, let it be done!

The Emperor's Games

Mother, Virgin, you wove in your womb
from purple silk
the robe of love made weak and poor:
have mercy now.

Master, we dare not enter your chamber
clad in rags:
O, Bridegroom, surpassing beauty,
clothe us with suffering.

O, blessed feet, O purest harlot's kiss,
behold, the feast is served.

Leave dungeon, chains.
We run, dazzled, between cheers and roars
to claim our prize.

Immoderate Conception

She sits unmoving, though the bairn inside,
restless, ripples her distended dress.
Dark eyes swim in her pale face.
Her hair is frizzed. The ends are split and dried.

Her mother, busy with necessities,
shops, saves coupons for a pram.
A few girl-friends, curious, still come.
She no longer fits their shape; embodies

their most secret fears, bulges
dread at what's ahead, yet finds the long wait hard.
"Three boys – turn about – out in the yard",
the mother says. "No proof who the father is.

She never said a word; we've only just been told."
The mother chain-smokes distress, stubs one word
against the next. The girl's thoughts are unheard:
fourteen, and heavy with thrice-fathered child.

A Woman Washing Clothes the Algarve, Portugal

Across sunlit railway tracks
in the shadow of a shack
a woman bends,
scrubs clothes on stone.
Opposite, three northern women shift
shoulders, throats towards the sun.
At home they wash with an automatic switch,
she rubs and wrings and twists. They watch;
distance diminishes: they feel at one.

Woman Poet: an Autobiography

The processes of birth,
nurture, growth
continue to adulthood

and beyond – through death.

Weighed down by *huswif*ry,
mothering,
I make my way
along tracks choked with dust,
impassable in parts, steep,
to the place where words which hurt
become metaphors of life.
I begin. I am. I have found me

in the melody which lies
at the core of being; is
laughter and loss
            drift
of sun across the face
of a child returning.

Identity

Wild lady of dreams,
Guinevere, Genevieve,
who betrayed her courteous king –
the breaking wave
washes your slender feet,
and Guinevere is Winifred
of the healing well. Apples swell
on gnarled boughs. Centuries reduce
the queen to fable and the saint to myth.
And I, who first saw this earth when war
rained death from darkened skies,
I hold you both –
Guinevere – Winifred
within the name my mother gave
to me at birth.

The Pattern

I hold a brown-veined autumn leaf,
a rose, a petal,
the patterning of growth and grief;
midwinter reft and dearth;
midnight vigil,
hope asleep; and feel
warmth beyond the snow,
a hidden path, lantern glow.

Shrieving

It is the eve of Lent. I sit
alone,
eating dark chocolate,
sipping wine;
thoughts turn within my mind:
words I would unsay.

The chocolate's a gift, the wine;
but mine
the memories, strewn
like crumpled washing round the room,

with ironing to be done,
and folded all, tidied away.

Rowans in Early August, Mid-Argyll

This month of low cloud, driving rain,
rowanberries star the sodden glen
like blood-apples, insignia of the absent sun,
whose bitter taste sours the throat and dries the questing tongue.

(Wild raspberries at the roadside stain
my mouth and fingers. Scratches score my arm.
Berries no gardener has grown
I garnish later with sugar, cream.)

But it is to rowans I turn
for potency enigmatic as a rune,
or rosary to twist out unspoken pain
when tears have turned to stone:
rowans whose bright beads gleam
as summer light dwindles, grows lean
and soft, sweet fruits are done.

Migrants

Two swallows flew north on eddies of air and wind,
knowing the route, the timing when
to start the flitting, trek from Sahara sand
to a green Argyll glen.
O, what strange stirring called them forth and guarded them?

Arrived, they bully small birds from the roof:
the squally air is loud with shrill protest.
Evicted ones disperse, displaced.
"The swallow," the Psalmist rejoiced,
"hath purchased in thy courts her nest."

Amidst spades and cobwebs, shears, old garden gloves
this pair have moulded mud into a house
within an unlocked shed, its key misplaced,
its owner at her cottage hearth weary with the weight
of years, gauging the time when she too should migrate...

Squatters, these, like the blackbird which wove
her nursery on a hermit's outstretched hand; unmoved
the patient brother held fledgling young unscathed.
"The King of All feedeth lion and songbird both,
and who am I but my Creator's slave?"

The birds fly in and out the open door, eggs laid.
Could such chance and casual lodgers, no rent paid,
be surety the mistress of the stead
will find safe tending as nights of four score years draw in?
Spring calls bright birds forth, but autumn bids them on.

Talitha, koum: a triptych

House facing winter

Choosing the sunshine, I try to forget
she's in the shadows, sleeping at noon-time;
try to find comfort in birdsong, waken each morning
to cadences carolled from branches and bushes around me
while she is shuttered in her summer of stupor,
a full-blown June rose, beautiful, blighted,
living with me in this house facing winter:
for the sun doesn't brighten our windows, visit our garden.

The wound in your mind

Rowanberries tinge the bright years of your lost girlhood.
You tell me beauty has a bitter taste.

A secret smile flickers across your face.
When you speak – your words are sharp with hurt.

The wound in your mind refuses love.

There is no key, you are locked in, fast.

The sea is a wild dream, a madness of foam.

If he hadn't looked at you, his eyes holding yours as he
spoke words of love. It was the look that took your heart,
the gentle words, praising your goodness.

You ordered your wedding dress, white as winter seas; held
lace finer than spindrift against your throat. The cloth is
half-sewn.

It is harder to mend a broken mind than make a satin dress.
Tangled thoughts twist fraying threads. The fabric crushes,
comes undone.

My swan princess... your lost self is lovelier than any dress.
Yours the pools and islands of the west:
fly again.

"O, the Owl is a baker's daughter..."

The mind, mind has mountains...
the self – caves.
You felt your pit-props slip;
and we only knew we'd lost you
into a twilit existence,
entombed in a bedroom grave.

Life has pricked you sore,
your mind's fingers bleed,

Briar Rose, bewitched princess...

Once you ran
over sunlit shores, sang
to seals, swam,
turned cartwheels across the sand

It was Eden, then.
Your fair hair shone in the westering sun;
we knew nothing of the night to come:
did not fear the snake.

The roses of your womanhood
are eaten with this blight; the garden
you once tended is overgrown with weeds

the music you danced to, the songs,
the friends you used to phone
all turned off, in this long
unfriendly silence.
No rosemary for remembrance;
no heart's ease – only rue.
The owl is a baker's daughter.
can young girl's wits be mortal?

> *I cast for comfort I can no more get,*
> never now see your blond head
> among the crowds in Princes Street
>
> among the crowds in Princes Street
> are folk in wheelchairs; guys who sit
> with placards, begging a meal, a bed,
>
> but your boots no longer stride, your head
> tosses on your pillows, haar or sun or wet
> *I cast for comfort... can no more get.*

You wept:
we listened to a litany of loss
day and night, night and day:
"No one can feel
what's happened to me. This is for real..."

When you were small
I carried you over cliffs,
laid you in a hollow,
that the earth might be your cradle,
April sun hold you;
you lay content,
eyes like quiet stars.

> *Talitha, koum...*
> I give you this rune:
> larksong restore you,
> warmth enfold you,
> love blossom again.

Aileen and baby
Heather